Impact of American Investment in India

Published by
ACADEMIC FOUNDATION
in association with

INDIAN COUNCIL FOR RESEARCH
ON INTERNATIONAL ECONOMIC
RELATIONS (ICRIER),
NEW DELHI

ABOUT THE AUTHORS

Saon Ray is Senior Fellow at Indian Council for Research on International Economic Relations (ICRIER), New Delhi. Her areas of interest include international trade, industrial economics, microeconomics and applied econometrics. She has a PhD in Economics from the Jawaharlal Nehru University (JNU), New Delhi, on the role of intellectual property rights in transferring technology to developing countries. She has worked in the area of trade policy, technology transfer, foreign direct investment, efficiency and productivity issues, behaviour of firms, energy and climate change related issues. She is currently engaged in projects that examine link between climate change adaptation and competitiveness of cities; and evaluating India's participation in global value chains. She has publications in various national and international journals as well as in edited books.

Smita Miglani is a Research Associate at ICRIER. Her broad areas of research interest include international/domestic trade and investment, energy and infrastructure studies. She is an MPhil in Economics from JNU. In the past, she has done studies in the areas of international trade and investment, climate change, renewable energy and transport sectors. Her work has contributed to India's negotiating strategies in signing bilateral trade and investment agreements and other policy reform issues at domestic level. She is currently engaged in projects that involve evaluating India's participation in global value chains. She has published work in working papers, edited books and refereed journals.

Neha Malik is a Research Associate at ICRIER. She completed her Masters in Economics from the University of Manchester, UK. She has worked on projects such as "The Macroeconomic Impact of Financial Crisis 2008-09: A Capital Account Analysis of Germany, India and Japan", "Impact of Transaction Taxes on Commodity Derivatives Trading", "Securities Transaction Tax in India: Motives, Revenues and Effects" and is currently involved in a project on "Covered Bonds: A Complementary Source of Financing Mortgage Lending in India". Her areas of interest include international finance, monetary and macroeconomic issues.

Impact of American Investment in India

A Socioeconomic Assessment

Saon Ray

Smita Miglani

Neha Malik

ACADEMIC FOUNDATION
NEW DELHI

www.academicfoundation.com

First published in 2014
by

ACADEMIC FOUNDATION
4772-73 / 23 Bharat Ram Road, (23 Ansari Road),
Darya Ganj, New Delhi - 110 002 (India).
Phones : 23245001 / 02 / 03 / 04.
Fax : +91-11-23245005.
E-mail : books@academicfoundation.com
www.academicfoundation.com

in association with
Indian Council for Research on International Economic Relations (ICRIER),
New Delhi.

Disclaimer:
The findings/views/opinions expressed in this book are solely those of the author and do not necessarily reflect the views of the publisher.

Cataloging in Publication Data--DK
Courtesy: D.K. Agencies (P) Ltd. <docinfo@dkagencies.com>

Ray, Saon.
Impact of American investment in India / Saon Ray, Smita Miglani, Neha Malik.
p. cm.
Includes bibliographical references (p.).
ISBN 9789332701458

1. Investments, American--Social aspects--India. 2. Investments, American--Economic aspects--India. I. Miglani, Smita, joint author. II. Malik, Neha, joint author. III. Title.

DDC 332.6730954 23

Typeset by Italics India, New Delhi.

Printed and bound by The Book Mint, New Delhi.
www.thebookmint.in

Contents

List of Tables, Boxes and Appendix

Tables

Boxes

Appendix

Appendix B

Appendix C: Questionnaires for Consumer Survey

Executive Summary

Executive Summary

The United States (US) is India's largest trade and investment partner and is engaged with India at various levels of economic cooperation. This study investigates the socio-economic impact of US direct investment in India and identifies the challenges faced by US investors. The study is based on secondary data and primary survey. Analysis of the secondary data helped in identifying sectors where the overall impact of US foreign direct investment (FDI) was high. A primary survey was then conducted in selected sectors, which comprised in-depth personal interviews and consultation meetings with relevant stakeholders.

We have matched the National Industrial Classification (NIC) codes used by the Department of Industrial Policy and Promotion (DIPP) with the North American Industrial Classification (NAIC) codes used by the Bureau of Economic Analysis (BEA) for each of the entries made by DIPP between 2004 and 2012 to arrive at the inflows from the USA. The largest recipient of US FDI in the last few years has been the services sector, followed by manufacturing. The sectors chosen for study in this report are finance, fast-moving consumer goods (FMCG), IT, pharmaceuticals, consulting and automobiles. They were chosen primarily because the spillovers (of the impact of investment) to the local/consumer level are relatively high. The primary survey of American firms and other stakeholders was carried out in Delhi/NCR, Mumbai, Bengaluru and Hyderabad in 2013.

The contribution of American investment is enormous: this study has not attempted to quantify it but has instead tried to highlight some of the most significant contributions as well as underline the channels through which they have come. The findings of the study include some examples of the direct impacts of American FDI. The employment generated by American firms in India is considerable. Exports from these firms are also significant. The indirect effects of American FDI need to be understood through generation of technology and spillovers thereof. Many American R&D centre in India are engaged in cutting-edge research, employ Indian scientists and engineers, and also transfer technology generated in these labs elsewhere. Best practices brought in by many of the American firms must be recognised.

1

Introduction

1

Introduction

The rapid pace of growth of the Indian economy over the last decade has led to increased global interest in it. Foreign investors have been keen to be part of that remarkable growth, one of the consequences of which was an increase inflow of funds/investment into the country. While investors gain from high returns on their investments, India benefits from the direct inflow of capital through creation of high quality jobs, transfer of technology and exports.

Inflow of funds can be in the form of either foreign institutional investment (FII) or foreign direct investment (FDI), the latter being the focus of this study. Net inflows of direct investment in India stood at US$ 32.2 billion in 2011.[1] The United States of America (USA)[2] is India's largest trade and investment partner and is engaged at various levels of economic cooperation. This study investigates the socioeconomic impact of US direct investment in India and identifies challenges faced by US investors in the country. This involves identifying sectors where US investment is relatively high followed by an assessment of consequent spillovers in the form of employment creation, contribution to exports, technology transfers, etc. The impact of FDI depends on many factors, such as the host country's policies and institutions, its labour laws and level of human capital, to name a few.

1. *World Development Indicators, 2013.*
2. Also referred to as 'the US' in this report.

2

Trends in FDI Inflows

2

Trends in FDI Inflows

2.1 Global Trends

Foreign direct investment (FDI) is defined as long-term investment by a non-resident with 10 per cent or more control. There are three components of FDI flows: cross-border mergers and acquisitions (M&As), greenfield projects and equity investment. Global FDI inflows fell by 18 per cent in 2012, as compared to the previous year. The drop was on account of a significant dip in FDI inflows in the developed economies. FDI inflows to developed economies fell by around 31 per cent between 2011 and 2012.

Developing countries accounted for more than half of global FDI in 2012, surpassing the developed economies for the very first time. This was driven largely by investments in Asia and Latin America. Investment in Asia, however, declined by 7 per cent in 2012 with South Asia witnessing the largest fall. India has continued to account for the bulk of inflows to South Asia. The FDI inflow into China has always been substantially larger than those into India.

2.2 Trends in India

FDI flows to India increased tremendously over the last decade indicating that it has become an attractive destination for foreign investors. Gross inflows of FDI to India increased from approximately US$ 5 billion in 2002-03 to US$ 46 billion in 2011-12.

India recently allowed full foreign ownership in parts of the agriculture sector, more specifically, in the development and production of seeds and planting material, animal husbandry, pisciculture, aquaculture under controlled conditions and services related to agribusiness and related sectors. In addition, the previous cap (51%) on foreign investment was removed to pave the way for a 100 per cent investment in single-brand retail. The Companies Act was amended in 2013—a snapshot of provisions that could affect FDI in the country is presented in Box 2.1.[1]

Box 2.1

The Companies Act 2013

The Companies Act, 2013 (2013 Act) was been published in India's Official Gazette on 30 August 2013. The 2013 Act replaces the Companies Act of 1956. It seeks to meet the needs of corporate bodies in India in the present global environment.

Some new definitions have been added to the Act including those of independent directors, and a one person company (OPC) with prescribed rights and provisions. New procedures and provisions for audit and accounting, corporate governance, inter-corporate loans/investments, and amalgamation and demergers have also been laid down.

Some provisions of the new Act that could affect FDI into the country are:

- Amalgamation of/demerger of Indian company from foreign company incorporated in a notified jurisdiction and vice versa allowed subject to approval of the Reserve Bank of India (RBI).
- Inability to pay debts to be considered as a criterion for classifying a company as sick.
- Government to establish serious Fraud Investigation Office for investigation of frauds relating to a company.
- Merger of Indian company with a foreign company allowed.
- The concept of corporate social responsibility (CSR) included in the statute of the Act and implies that every company having a net worth of Rs. 5 billion or more, or a turnover of Rs. 10 billion or more, or a net profit of Rs. 50 million or more, during any financial year shall be liable to ensure that in every financial year, it has to spend at least two per cent of its average net profits during the three immediate preceding financial years in pursuance of its CSR policy.

1. Details of the Act are available at *http://www.mca.gov.in/Ministry/pdf/CompaniesAct2013.pdf* (Last accessed on 23/10/2013).

Some major countries investing in India include the United States, Japan and Germany. Although Mauritius is the largest investor in terms of value of FDI inflows, the US surpasses other leading investors in terms of number of FDI projects.[2] The source-wise investment in terms of value of FDI is presented in Table 2.1.

Examining the inflows of FDI from USA based on data from the Department of Industrial Policy and Promotion (DIPP) (shown in Appendix Table A.1), we note that there is a discrepancy between the FDI data reported as inflows by DIPP, and outflows reported by the Bureau of Economic Analysis (BEA) (shown in Appendix Table A.2).[3]

The classification adopted by the two agencies is also different: the DIPP uses the National Industrial Classification (NIC) classification, while the BEA uses the North American Industry Classification (NAIC). We have tried to match the NIC codes with the NAIC codes for each of the entries made by the DIPP between 2004 and 2012 to arrive at Appendix Table A.1. Some sectors in the two tables have similar entries. For example, the chemicals sector records an inflow of US$ 319.36 million according to the DIPP in 2007 (Appendix Table A.1), while outflows, according to the BEA, in the same sector for the same year are US$ 375 million.

The largest recipients of FDI in the last few years have been the services sector followed by manufacturing. Sectors with the largest US FDI inflows during 2004-2012 were financial services, food and beverages (within manufacturing), and construction. This is in conformity with the general pattern of FDI inflows in India. Most countries exhibit this pattern except South Korea, from which inflows to India into the manufacturing sector are greater than those into the services sector (Ray and Kaushal, 2012).

---

2. Ernst & Young (2012) "Ready for the Transition", Attractiveness Survey, India. A large part of the FDI from Mauritius is by American firms.

3. FDI recorded by DIPP is invariably lower compared to data from RBI (Rajan *et al.*, 2011).

Table 2.1

Foreign Direct Investment Inflows by Origin for Selected Countries*

(US$ million)

	2006-07	*2007-08*	*2008-09*	*2009-10*	*2010-11*	*2011-12*	*2012-13*	*2013-14*[a]
Mauritius	6363	11096	11229	10376	6987	9942	9497	4113
Singapore	578	3073	3454	2379	1705	5257	2308	3678
US	856	1089	1802	1943	1170	1115	557	721
UK	1878	1177	864	657	2711	7874	1080	3187
Netherlands	644	695	883	899	1213	1409	1856	1700
Japan	85	815	405	1183	1562	2972	2237	1009
Cyprus	58	834	1287	1627	913	1587	490	464
Germany	120	514	629	626	200	1622	860	849
France	117	145	467	303	734	663	646	288
UAE	260	258	257	629	341	353	180	230
Total inflows, based on equity capital components	12492	24575	27330	25834	21383	35121	22423	18749

Note: * Equity inflows; a data upto January 2014.

Source: Compiled from various factsheets on FDI of the DIPP, Government of India.

The sectors chosen for study in this report are the finance/ banking, fast-moving consumer goods (FMCG), information technology (IT), pharmaceuticals, consulting, automobiles and others.[4]

4. 'Others' here represents industries such as paper, chemicals, e-commerce and education.

3

Socioeconomic Impact of US Investment in India

3

Socioeconomic Impact of US Investment in India

3.1 Impact of FDI

There are many dimensions of the impact of foreign direct investment (FDI) on host countries since FDI has direct and indirect effects on the host economy. The direct effects are often measured in terms of employment generation, skill upgradation, economic growth, etc. Indirect effects can be in the form of transfer of technology which further raises the level of research and development (R&D), productivity of domestic firms, etc. The effect of FDI on growth depends on factors such as infrastructure, business environment, and critical level of human capital, in the host country.

3.2 Methodology

The study is based upon the results of a primary survey and upon secondary data. Secondary data was analysed to help identify sectors where the overall impact of US FDI was high. A primary survey was then conducted in selected sectors; 40 in-depth personal interviews and consultation meetings with relevant stakeholders were held in each sector. The survey was carried out in Delhi/NCR,[1] Mumbai (Maharashtra), Bengaluru (Karnataka) and Hyderabad (Andhra Pradesh) during April-September 2013.[2]

---

1. NCR stands for national capital region.
2. The FDI regime in selected sectors is given in Appendix Table A.3. The survey also examined the barriers faced by US firms in investing in India. As mentioned earlier, the selected sectors include auto and auto components, finance/banking, fast-moving consumer goods (FMCG), IT, health care and pharmaceuticals. A snapshot is presented in Appendix Table B.1. The questionnaire used in the survey is reproduced in Appendix B.

3.3 Findings from the Survey

The direct effect of FDI is felt at the level of the firm or company since it allows for construction of new facilities or plants, acquisition of equipment and supplies, and hiring/training of workers. This section outlines, broadly, findings from the survey.

Inputs of the individual (surveyed) companies comprising a particular sector have been collated to arrive at a broader sectoral view, in some cases. Some companies' names have been withheld upon request. A brief summary of the impact of American FDI on selected sectors is given in Table 3.1.[3]

Table 3.1

Impact of American FDI on Selected Sectors

Sector-wise	*Contribution*
Automobile and auto components	• Manufacturing of high-end automobiles
Banking and Finance	• Vast network of online banking and promotion of plastic money
Bio-technology	• R&D; development of hybrid seeds
Consulting	• Promotion of outsourcing activity
FMCG	• Organisation of supply chain networks
IT	• Promotion of outsourcing activity
Pharmaceuticals	• Diversification of presence across segments and access to high-efficacy drugs
All sectors	• Corporate best-practices • Revenue and employment generation

Source: Authors' compilation based on socioeconomic survey.

3.3.1 Automobile and Auto Components Sector

3.3.1.1 Socioeconomic Survey

Ford India Private Limited and General Motors India Private Limited are two US-based automobile companies with a significant

3. More details of the survey can be found in a forthcoming ICRIER working paper on the same issue.

presence in India. Both of them have vehicle manufacturing facilities and engine plants in the country.

The operations of Ford India Private Limited also include Global Business Services, which comprise a Business Services Centre, and Ford Technology Services Centre located in Chennai (Tamil Nadu), Coimbatore (Tamil Nadu) and Delhi. These centres support Ford's global operations in the areas of IT, accounting and finance, automotive operations support, global analytics, and engineering services.

General Motors India Private Limited has a technical centre in Bangalore which is involved in engineering, design and R&D activities for developing alternative, environment friendly technologies of the future.

The presence of other American companies in the auto component sector is also significant. These firms have manufacturing plants at locations in Tamil Nadu, Gujarat, Maharashtra and the NCR.

Box 3.1

Delphi

Delphi India was incorporated in 1995 as a wholly owned subsidiary of Delphi and specializes in the design and production of a wide range of automotive products and electronics. It operates in several locations, and has manufacturing facilities in Chennai, Gurgaon (Haryana), Dharuhera (Haryana) and Greater Noida (Uttar Pradesh), a technical centre in Bangalore (Karnataka) and the Delphi-TVS joint venture in Chennai.

Delphi provides original equipment quality parts and services to the Indian aftermarket. It supplies products to major original equipment manufacturers in India and also exports to North America. The company provides employment to a diverse local workforce trained at facilities both in India and abroad.

Source: Authors' compilation.

Some of these firms manufacture a wide array of components while others have their own assembly units and also serve as original equipment manufacturers (OEMs) for automobile manufacturing companies. These companies have brought in the latest technologies and some of them are exploring the possibility of manufacturing for export markets.

One of the automobile companies has a technical centre in Bangalore, which is actively involved in research, design, analysis and development of vehicles for both the global and the Indian market.

3.3.2 The Financial/Banking Sector

The Indian financial sector comprises commercial banks, financial services and/or non-banking financial companies (NBFCs), stock exchanges, and insurance. The primary survey in this sector focused on banking and related financial services.

3.3.2.1. Socioeconomic Survey

The findings suggest that American banks are usually wholly owned subsidiaries of the parent company as has been prescribed by the Reserve Bank of India (RBI).[4] Some American banks have also set up NBFC entity/(ies) such as wealth and/or asset management businesses and investment advisory services.

All three entities, banking, non-banking and sourcing, have generated significant employment opportunities. The impact has been particularly important in the area of sourcing operations. Table 3.2 is a snapshot of some of the firms surveyed.

4. The questionnaire used for this survey is reproduced in Appendix B.

Table 3.2

Summary of Findings

	Operations	*Employment*	*Technology/Skill Upgradation*	*Liquidity*
Citibank	Banking and non-banking. Within non-banking, sourcing operations.	7500	Established Iflex Solutions Limited and Citigroup Global Services Limited (CGSL). Oracle acquired Iflex in 2005 and CGSL was acquired by Tata Consultancy Services (TCS) in 2008.	Significant liquidity generated through transient funds.
Bank of America	Banking and non-banking. Within non-banking, sourcing operations.	700 in banking and 20,000 in sourcing	Skill upgradation due to continuous interaction with the parent company	Significant liquidity generated
Northern Operating Services Limited	Only sourcing operations	1/3rd of global workforce	Skill upgradation with respect to fixed income research	Not applicable
Others (names withheld on request)	Asset management and sourcing	Significant	Knowledge upgradation due to continuous interaction with the parent company	Liquidity generated through asset management. Not applicable to NBFCs with sourcing operations.

Source: Authors' compilation based on socioeconomic survey.

3.3.3 FMCG Sector

FMCG forms the fourth largest sector in the Indian economy and it is expected to grow to US$ 74 billion by the year 2018. Up to 100 per cent foreign equity is allowed in single retail brands[5] and up to 51 per cent of foreign equity is allowed in multi-brand retail. The market is highly fragmented and almost 50 per cent of the share is taken up by unbranded, unpackaged home-made products.

The survey focused on six categories of FMCG products: skin care, hair care, detergent powder, cold drinks, toothpaste and packaged food. American companies also sell consumer products directly in India. Some well-known names in the FMCG sector are Procter & Gamble Company (foods, cleaning agents and personal care products), PepsiCo Inc. (food and beverages), Coca-Cola Company (beverages) and Amway (direct selling of homecare and personal care products).

3.3.3.1 Socioeconomic Survey

American companies have entered the Indian market and are performing well in each of these segments (the questionnaire used is given in Appendix B.2).

Existing companies in the FMCG sector in India have established themselves in the market and are currently consolidating their portfolios. Amway India offers over 130 products in five products categories such as personal care, home care, nutrition and wellness, cosmetics, etc. Amway India manufactures almost all products within the country through third party contract manufacturers and transfer of technology has taken place. By contrast, companies such as Procter & Gamble and Dupont are industrial groups and sell multiple products.

Product customisation is being offered by companies to attract a wider range of customers. The products meet global quality

5. Approvals for investments are almost automatic.

standards. The companies have brought in corporate best practices. Companies have also invested in supply chain management to reach deeper into the rural markets. They provide employment to several thousand people.

3.3.4 IT Sector

The Indian IT sector can be divided into three major segments: software, IT services and ITeS-BPO (IT enabled services-business process outsourcing). These can further be divided into sub-segments. The software segment can be divided into software products and engineering and R&D services. The IT services segment can be divided into project-oriented services (IT consulting, systems integration, core architecture data model, network consulting and integration, and software testing), core IT outsourcing services (application management, outsourcing and web or e-commerce services), and training and support services. The ITeS-BPO segment includes client interaction, financing and accounting, human resource (HR), and knowledge process outsourcing (KPO) services.

3.3.4.1 Socioeconomic Survey[6]

Multinational corporations (MNCs) of the US origin are present in all segments of the IT industry. According to the National Association of Software and Services Companies (NASSCOM) (2010), the US was the biggest market for the Indian BPO industry, accounting for a major share, 60.4 per cent of the total BPO exports in 2010. Many companies such as Mphasis started with a BPO arm and later moved on to software application development in the infrastructure sector. The survey sample for this study covered a few firms in all segments.

American investment has been critical to the IT industry. It has provided a tremendous boost, bringing in capital and technology.

6. The questionnaire used in this segment is reproduced in Appendix B.

Other significant benefits include employment generation and improved HR skills.

Companies such as Dell have also set up an assembling and R&D centre in India in addition to captive BPO, sales and marketing, financial services, and analytics and software services. Similarly, Microsoft Corporation operates through six business units in India and has been able to contribute significantly to employment (5,800 people) and sharpen HR skills.

Box 3.2

Microsoft

Microsoft was one of the first foreign companies to set up base in India's IT sector in 1990;it has been a key IT partner to the Indian government, academia and the local developer community. In 1998, it set up its second software development center outside the U.S. (the first was in Israel), in Hyderabad, Andhra Pradesh leading the way for other such companies in the city. Microsoft India (R&D) Private Limited set up the Microsoft India Development Center (MSIDC) at Hyderabad in 1998, which has expanded to become one of Microsoft Corporation's largest R&D centers outside its headquarters in Redmond.

The company runs six business units in India: Microsoft Corporation India (Private) Ltd (the marketing division); Microsoft India Development Center; Microsoft Global Technical Support Centre; Microsoft IT; Microsoft Services Global Delivery; and, Microsoft Research India. Altogether these represent the complete Microsoft product lifecycle. It has offices in nine Indian cities: Ahmedabad, Bangalore, Chennai, Hyderabad, Kochi, Kolkata, Mumbai, New Delhi and Pune; and employs about 5,800 people in the country.

Source: Compiled from various sources by authors.

US investment is, however, inclined more towards the Indian software segment as compared to hardware, in terms of manufacturing and R&D units. Likewise, exports from the software and services segments are higher.

OSI Systems was set up in India around the year 2001 and has a R&D centre. ECIL-RAPISCAN has supplied X-ray baggage/cargo inspection systems (XBIS) to Indian customers such as the customs, airports authority, Parliament House, defence, air lines and state police.

Automatic Data Processing (ADP) India provides IT and ITeS to ADP's business divisions worldwide, specifically to HR services and dealership services. IT services are provided in Europe, India and Asia Pacific.

According to NASSCOM (2010), India's contribution to new patents in the world is less than one per cent. The Indian IT industry needs to develop innovative solutions in climate change, mobile software applications, clinical research, automotive platform development, cloud-computing technology-enabled health care delivery and economical medical device designs.

3.3.5. The Pharmaceutical Sector

The Indian pharmaceutical industry is third largest in the world in terms of volume. Since the introduction of product patents, there has been considerable inflow of foreign investment in this sector, specifically investment by US companies. Some of the American pharmaceutical giants present in India include Pfizer Inc., Merck Inc., Mylan Inc. and Abbott Laboratories.[7]

3.3.5.1. Socioeconomic Survey

Many US pharmaceutical companies have entered the Indian market and partnered with Indian companies in almost all segments of this industry. They have entered into alliances with local generic pharmaceutical companies to jointly manufacture and market drugs.

---

7. In 2013, India decided that FDI proposals for M&As in the pharmaceutical sector would have to pass through the government approval route, and would no longer pass through the 'automatic' route. This decision was made to ensure a balance between public health concerns and attracting FDI in the sector.

For instance, Pfizer has entered into an alliance with Aurobindo Pharma to market drugs in offshore markets.

Novavax Inc., a clinical-stage pharmaceutical company, has a joint venture with the Indian company, Cadila Pharmaceuticals, for development and manufacturing of vaccines and other bio-pharmaceutical products in India.

In the year 2009, U.S.-based Mylan signed a deal with India's Biocon to develop, manufacture, supply and commercialise many high-value generic biologic compounds for global markets.

US companies are also active in the over-the-counter (OTC) drug market. For instance, Pfizer launched Listerine, Benadryl, Caladryl and Benylin in India which were later sold to Johnson and Johnson Limited. India serves as the manufacturing location for OTC products for exports to other markets.

OTC manufacturer Perrigo started its operations in India in the year 2003, initially focusing on supporting global sourcing of active pharmaceutical ingredients. Gradually, they entered into the areas of formulation and analytical R&D, quality assurance, external auditing and sourcing.

Other segments where U.S. companies are present include research and conducting clinical trials. U.S. pharma research organisations such as Quintiles, Omnicare Inc. and Pharma-Olam International have operations in India. U.S. companies have also made forays into the niche segment of stem cell research. For instance, StemCyte India Therapeutics Private Limited (SCITPL) is a joint venture between StemCyte Inc. (USA), Apollo Hospital Enterprises Limited and Cadila Pharmaceuticals Limited. Pfizer and Eli Lilly and Company are among the MNCs which have been conducting clinical tests in India for some time.

3.3.6 Consulting

Consulting services sector in India can be broadly categorised into management consultancy and engineering consultancy. Over the last few years, India's consultancy sector has grown rapidly owing to factors such as liberalisation of the FDI regime and cost arbitrage. The focal point of this survey was American companies in India's management consultancy market which comprises mainly of companies involved in accountancy and other professional services such as audit, assurance, tax and advisory. The IT/engineering consulting firms have not been included in this section.

3.3.6.1 Socioeconomic Survey

Consulting firms which are established brands such as Price Waterhouse Coopers (PWC), KPMG, Ernst & Young (E&Y) and Deloitte operate under specific industry and services verticals.

These firms have generated significant employment opportunities. PWC, KPMG, E&Y and Deloitte together account for approximately 37,000 employees across India. Some of the best practices of Deloitte include streamlining career and HR management, knowledge transmission (from the parent company) in the form of in-person connects, leadership programmes, etc. The export unit of Deloitte accounts for almost 10 per cent of the revenue of the global business.

Since research and communication skills are important concerns for most of these companies, they also take initiatives such as skill upgradation and training programmes. In Corporate Executive Board, a career committee is appointed which ensures downward and upward review calibration so as to eliminate any element of bias in the process of appraisal.

3.3.7 Prominent Players Impacting India's Growth Story

Apart from firms in the selected sectors, a few other American companies were also surveyed. The criteria for their inclusion were the size of investment (present and prospective), as well as their economic importance. Of these, there were some which had yet to establish or had a negligible presence in India.

3.3.7.1 Companies with a Presence in India

General Electric (GE), a firm that operates in several segments such as energy, health care, aviation and transportation, was also surveyed. This firm manages its health care manufacturing and renewable energy segment *via* joint ventures with Indian entities.

It employs 15,000 people in the country of which about 4,000-5,000 are in its R&D center. This centre caters to global needs and is involved in developing cutting edge products. About 10-15 per cent of manufactured products are exported from India.

International Paper is a US manufacturer of paper and packaging products and entered the Indian market in 2011; it is a 100 per cent subsidiary of the US parent. Some benefits of the investment have been in the form of significant technology spillover from the US parent in terms of improving the strength and quality of paper. The company is also looking ahead to setting up a greenfield project for 'kraft' paper.

Huber is, a US company, in the business of chemicals and additives in India. It started its operations as a joint venture in 1991 and became a 100 per cent owned company in the year 1994, when it set up a manufacturing facility in Gujarat. The company supplies to the oral care, paints and coatings, beverage (fruit juices and jams), and paper industries. Companies such as Colgate Palmolive India Limited, Unilever and GlaxoSmithKline Pharmaceuticals Limited (GSK) are their customers. About 55 per cent of its manufactured products are exported to the South East, Middle East, Egypt, Thailand, Vietnam and Turkey.

3.3.7.2 Companies with Negligible Presence/Prospective Plans

PayPal Inc. is a US e-commerce business-based service allowing payments and money transfers without sharing financial information.

They have established an offshore office in India, which employs around 100 people. This office and its operations are essentially aimed at providing customer support in order to maintain their existing products.

Millennial Media Inc. is a leading American independent mobile advertising and data platform powering the app economy. They have a presence in India but this remains negligible due to lack of a well-developed market in the absence of a large base of smart phone users.

William Scotsman Inc. is a US company that makes, leases, sells and manages mobile offices and is considering the Indian market as they see a large demand for their products, especially in the construction sector.

The company is currently in the phase of analysing the logistics of providing modular spaces in India. In addition, they also aim to start a pilot project in the suburbs of Mumbai that will allow them to study the feasibility of entering the Indian market.

Counterpoint Consultants (India) LLP is a provider of enterprise software solutions. It provides advisory services such as vendor selection and management and programme remediation for offshoring programmes.

The company has made no significant investments in India but hires a local workforce to work at their head office in Virginia (USA). The reason is the absence of a large market in India for their cloud- and mobile-based business automation solutions.

3.3.8 Consumer Survey

Apart from this, a socioeconomic survey was also carried out at the local level to assess the perception of the general public on the impact of American companies in India. This survey was conducted for four sectors, the FMCG, IT, pharmaceutical and banking. These sectors were chosen primarily because spillovers (of the impact of investment) to the local/consumer level are relatively high in their case.[8] Table 3.3 highlights some of the findings.

Table 3.3

Findings from the Consumer Survey

Sector	*Findings*
IT	• Wide use of web browsers and office suites • Quality assured with warranty (even though price is higher)
Banking/finance	• Huge impact on employment but do not have a large customer base
FMCG	• Better quality though expensive • Cosmetics and detergents more popular than other products
Pharmaceuticals	• Significant impact though drug prices are higher

Source: Authors' compilation based on consumer survey.

3.4 Summing up

The contributions and the impact of American FDI in India are shown in Table 3.4.

Table 3.4

Main Areas of Operation of American Firms

Sector	*Area of Operation*
IT	• Mainly outsourcing operations • Software development and management
Banking/finance	• Outsourcing operations—advisory services, asset management solutions • Data and risk management • Client reporting • Credit research
Consultancy	• Solution designing • Project management
Pharmaceuticals	• Manufacturing of branded generics • Health care equipment

Source: Authors' compilation based on socioeconomic survey.

8. The questionnaires drafted for the chosen sectors are reproduced as Appendix C.

As apparent from Appendix Table B.1, the employment provided by American firms in India is considerable. American firms have set up manufacturing facilities as well as R&D centres in the country and are engaged in state-of-the-art technology development. Exports from these firms are also considerable. Table 3.5 summarises some of the problems faced by the firms in each of the sectors surveyed.

Table 3.5

Key Problems Faced

Sector	*Problems*
IT	• Taxation and regulatory delays • Arbitrariness in procedures • Unclear regulations (w.r.t. setting up businesses, transfer pricing)
Banking/finance	• Regulatory concerns
Pharmaceuticals	• Weak intellectual property rights (IPR) regime • Unclear regulations on clinical trials
Automobile and auto components	• Infrastructure-related concerns

Source: Authors' compilation based on socioeconomic survey.

One of the objectives of surveying consulting firms was to gather details of their vertical on tax/transfer pricing. The issue of transfer pricing has been a major stumbling block for most foreign companies that have already set up their subsidiaries in India and has also hindered potential investment by other companies.

Table 3.6 presents some of the key areas of corporate social responsibility (CSR) activities of the American firms in India.

Table 3.6

Key Areas of CSR Activities

Sector	*Areas*
Chemical manufacturing	Mainly embedded in working practices • Employment of locals • Strict about following environmental norms • Train workmen on safety standards
FMCG	Embedded in working practices
Consultancy firms	• Employees teaching at local schools
Finance	• Community service • Individual-driven donations/ local charities • Partnership with other non-government organisations (NGOs) • Investment in welfare promoting funds

Source: Authors' compilation based on socioeconomic survey.

4

Conclusion

4

Conclusion

The contribution of American investment is enormous. While the study has not attempted to quantify such contributions, it highlights some of the most significant ones as well as underlines the channels through which these contributions are transmitted. As mentioned in the introduction to the study, the overall contribution of investment has to be seen in terms of direct impacts such as creation of jobs as well as indirect impacts such as the spillover effects of the R&D on growth. While some examples of the direct impacts of American FDI have been mentioned in the study, the indirect effects through generation of technology also need to be understood. Most American R&D centres in India are engaged in cutting edge research, employ Indian scientists and engineers, and also transfer technology generated in these labs elsewhere. The best practices brought in by many of the American firms also must be recognised. Notwithstanding the problems faced by American MNCs in India, most have indicated that they are here for the long term.

References

References

Italian Trade Commission (2008). *The Cosmetic & Personal Care Sector in India*. Market Research on India's Cosmetics and Personal Care Sector. Italian Trade Commission.

KPMG (2006). *The Indian Pharmaceutical Industry: Collaboration for Growth*. (Last accessed on 20/10/13.)

NASSCOM (2010). "The IT-BPO Sector in India", *Strategic Review 2010*. NASSCOM.

PWC (2010). "Global Pharma Looks to India: Prospects for Growth", *http://www.pwc.com/en_GX/gx/pharma-life-sciences/pdf/global-pharma-looks-to-india.pdf* (Last accessed on 20/10/2013).

———. (2013). "The Indian FMCG Sector: The Innovation Imperative", February. *http://www.pwc.in/en_IN/in/assets/pdfs/rc-publications/innovation-in-fmcg.pdf* (Last accessed on 12/12/2013).

Rajan, R.S., S. Rongala, R. Ghosh and S. Ray (2011). "Inward Foreign Direct Investment (FDI) and External Policy", in Santosh Kumar (ed.), *In the National Interest: A Companion Volume*. Business Standard Books.

Ray, S. and N. Kaushal (2012). "Investment in the Indo-Korea CEPA", in P. Shome and C.Y. Ahn (eds.), *Korea-India: Deepening Partnerships for the 21st Century*. Seoul: KIEP and SFIA.

The World Bank (2013). *World Development Indicators*. *http://databank.worldbank.org/data/download/WDI-2013-ebook.pdf* (Last accessed on 10/09/2013).

Articles

http://articles.economictimes.indiatimes.com/2012-05-02/news/31538420_1_natco-pharma-torrent-pharma-aurobindo-pharma

http://www.financialexpress.com/news/a-cure-for-pills/1114549

http://www.financialexpress.com/news/clinical-trials-swallowing-a-bittersweet-pill/1114550/4

http://www.financialexpress.com/news/drug-bans-all-talk-no-walk/1114551

Appendix

Appendix A

Table A.1

FDI Inflows from USA to India

(US$ million)

			2004	2005	2006	2007	2008	2009	2010	2011	2012	Total
Mining	Gas		42.29	10.46	71.75	117.33	1031	400	350.67	297.08	231.7	2552.71
Construction			92.59	223.43	936.78	3110.9	3157	3043	551.07	2566.13	2013	15693.48
Manufacturing	Food and Beverages		9.48	188.97	49.24	109.9	558.3	398	6060.2	273.1	18494	26140.89
	Chemical		32	39.68	81.53	319.36	259.7	212	24.4	113.06	158.9	1240.66
	Metal, plastic and rubber		4.83	120.94	169.18	536.17	890.5	499.4	6.77	525.63	768.9	3522.39
	Computers IT		125.95	245.94	1338.7	2195.6	815.8	736.7	219.6	880.25	194.1	6752.72
	Electric, electronics		6.68	35.29	50.89	508.78	252.3	244	94.07	1480.33	203.3	2875.69
	Glass		5.81	0.74	3.09	19.95	39.91	24.63	2.16	26.15	57.48	179.92
	Machine tools		3.86	57.21	64.81	180.99	118.2	302.2	8.54	292.18	397	1425
	Leather		0.04	1.48	1.22	8.36	2.78	2.44	0	7.63	14.84	38.79
	Transportation Equipment	Auto	0	12.23	7.01	10.6	41.5	40.78	679.94	44.92	35.3	872.28
		Aircraft	0	0	0.44	12.92	0.51	0.49	0	10.3	4.14	28.8
		Ship boat	0.18	36.51	36.11	87.15	25.23	268.9	193.98	12.39	8.36	668.77
	Engine			0.78	12.37	56.64	79.83	104.4	20.57	262.73	230.6	767.91
	Fertilisers and pesticides			63.23	112.67	33.67	108.4	24.23	3.58	51.7	62.45	459.9
	Wire cables			30.65	2.96	27.51	236.4	121.5	0.92	114.55	3.98	538.53
	Cycle			8.07	4.3	76.41	42.1	348.6	0.38	237.91	17.78	735.52

contd...

...contd...

		2004	*2005*	*2006*	*2007*	*2008*	*2009*	*2010*	*2011*	*2012*	*Total*
	Wood furniture	0.28	0.47	1.9	0.82	5.68	7.32	0.1	12.55	54.17	83.29
	Sanitary, cosmetics and jewellery	2.89	11.53	69.78	20.02	55.33	41.79	24.55	207.26	131	564.12
	Animal dairy products			1.53	81.12	13.27	2.43	12.08	6.69	10.07	127.19
	Bearings		7.43	10.73	29.22	24.34	31.86	16.74	36.7		157.02
	Medical	3.2	107.79	224.4	252.49	320.9	271.1	117.54	3275.44	426.2	4999.07
	Cereals, pulses, oils	0.05	0.06			0.25	5.36		41.22	9.93	56.87
	Textiles	16.38	79.27	124.83	345.54	188.6	503.9	107.72	225.98	277.8	1870.06
	Cement, ceramics	25.94	447.76	215.88	118.58	992.7	76.11	230.88	229.99	155.9	2493.76
	Telephones	9.84	0.01		0.37		4.08		19.91		34.21
Agriculture, forestry, fishing and hunting	Horticulture and nursery	0.49			0.5	1.84	0.37		6.49	12.44	22.13
Administrative and support and waste management and remediation services	Tours and travel	12.89	1.02	6.59	61.08	79.96	110.6	23.74	61.44	31.31	388.67
Healthcare and social assistance		1.59	69.92	31.23	280.7	219	52.62	4.75	136.6	410.6	1206.99
Transportation and Warehousing	Transportation	39.55	143.78	324.02	336.27	689.5	677.5	174.3	1144.83	3328	6857.33
	Warehousing		0	0.79	9.72	95.47	3.28		249.24	17.92	376.42
	Courier services		121.21	0.3	121.79	91.13	44.02	14.28	27.37	9.19	429.29

contd...

...contd...

		2004	2005	2006	2007	2008	2009	2010	2011	2012	Total
Information	Movie broadcasting	0.08	20.8	86.99	304.04	227.1	934	554.45	180.21	385.1	2692.8
	Telephone		106.78	382.23	1622.6	2044	2535	1685.3	1636.39	44.26	
Utilities	Gas	42.29	10.46	71.75	117.33	1031	400	350.67	297.08	231.7	8341.06
	Electricity	3.36	24.37	377.29	682.83	1120	1857	1084.5	1924.47	1267	164.17
Finance		111.65	1024.7	2902.7	3632.5	6000	5557	790.62	3321.54	2896	26237.31
Real estate and rental and leasing		0.21	14.93	455.48	788.28	1651	2695	1.28	234.57	246.4	6086.59
Professional services	Architectural	0.07	13.59	3.38	2.12	23.8	46.26	4.18	46.28	24.49	164.17
	Advertising	0.14	1.53	6.01	8.79	51.52	22.09	5.74	89.18	127.9	312.87
	Business and management	33.95	21.3	75.88	27.95	82.36	287.6	14.34	134.51	71.35	749.19
	Human Resource	1.93	4.12	5.27	8.87	12.72	14.85	0	23.33	12.63	83.72
	Marketing		0.44	4.5	2.88	44.25	122.8	5.2	17.74	30.44	228.2
	Research	2.75	4.42	68.62	138.82	78.58	1229	16.99	63.97	38.56	1641.22
Education		0.02	4.48	41.08	3.65	236.4	61.97	0.61	75.58	194.5	618.31
Other categories											
BPO_KPO		4.8	9.85	54.82	118.87	367.2	181.2	45.35	277.32	4.35	1063.71
Bed cover, curtains dye		0.03	0.79	0.36	1.98	4.19	9.1	2.33	4.27	0.68	23.73
Furnace Heat Management			0.28		1.07	0.19	20.49	0	15.12	29.11	66.26
Commissioning Agents			0	0.23	0	19.77	9.47		7.91	27.32	64.7
Advisory Consultancy			3.4	3.34	0.38	35.34	40.15	0.28	1.94	1.14	85.97

Note: Based on data from DIPP based on NIC classification and matched for each inflow with NAIC classification followed by BEA.

Source: Authors' compilation.

Table A.2

US FDI Outflows to India

(US$ million)

		2006	2007	2008	2009	2010	2011	2012
All Industries Total		1834	3915	4310	2470	3069	2023	4116
Mining		-8	145	(D)	118	185	(D)	(D)
Utilities		n.s.	n.s.	n.s.	n.s	n.s	n.s	n.s
Manufacturing	Total Manufacturing	398	577	827	75	193	224	656
	Food	-2	-1	-49	15	-41	8	7
	Chemicals	76	375	171	-97	-28	-239	597
	Primary and fabricated metals	(D)	(D)	(D)	-1	10	14	3
	Machinery	54	160	111	145	187	147	1
	Computers and electronic products	68	-55	193	81	31	-37	-50
	Electrical equipment, appliances and components	85	36	-77	-131	120	88	74
	Transportation equipment	(D)	(D)	410	-29	-146	105	-18
	Other manufacturing	(D)	(D)	(D)	93	60	138	43
Wholesale trade		133	66	248	93	201	149	33
Information		287	1749	570	71	300	328	559
Depository institutions		102	190	(D)	(D)	(D)	(D)	(D)
Finance (except depository institutions) and insurance		202	543	1081	688	210	68	356
Professional, scientific and technical services		748	356	874	1041	1525	1230	1596
Holding companies (non-bank)		30	-10	-84	23	35	(D)	(D)
Other industries		-58	299	(D)	(D)	(D)	(D)	(D)

Notes: (1) US Direct Investment Abroad, Financial outflows without current cost adjustment

(2) (D) indicates that the data in the cell have been suppressed to avoid disclosure of data of individual companies. Prior to 2006, income is presented net of U.S. and foreign withholding taxes. Beginning with 2006, income is presented gross of U.S. and foreign withholding taxes.

Source: U.S. BEA.

Table A.3

FDI Regime in Selected Sectors

Sector	*FDI Cap/Equity*	*Entry Route*	*Other Conditions*
1. Manufacturing			
(i) Hazardous chemicals and isocyanates	100 per cent	Automatic	
(ii) Industrial explosives—manufacture	100 per cent	Automatic	
(iii) Drugs and Pharmaceuticals	100 per cent	Automatic	
(FDI is not permitted in generation, transmission and distribution of electricity produced in atomic power plants/atomic energy since private investment in this activity is prohibited and reserved for public sector.)			
2. Asset reconstruction companies	49 per cent	FIPB	
3. Banking (private) sector	74 per cent (FDI+FII). FII not > 49 per cent	Automatic	
4. NBFCs: underwriting, portfolio management services, investment advisory services, financial consultancy, stock broking, asset management, venture capital, custodian, factoring, leasing and finance, housing finance, forex broking, etc.	100 per cent	Automatic	Subject to minimum capitalisation norms
6. Commodity exchanges	49 per cent (FDI+FII) (FDI 26 per cent FII 23 per cent)	FIPB	

contd...

...contd...

Sector	*FDI Cap/Equity*	*Entry Route*	*Other Conditions*
7. Insurance	26 per cent	Automatic	Clearance from IRDA
ISP with gateways, radio paging, end-to-end bandwidth.	74 per cent	Automatic—up to 49 per cent FIPB—beyond 49 per cent up to 74 per cent	
ISP without gateways	74 per cent	Automatic—up to 49 per cent FIPB—beyond 49 per cent up to 74 per cent	
Infrastructure provider providing dark fibre, right of way, duct space, tower (Category I)	100 per cent	100 per cent (Automatic—up to 49 per cent) (FIPB—beyond 49 per cent)	
Electronic and voice mail	100 per cent	100 per cent (Automatic—up to 49 per cent) (FIPB—beyond 49 per cent)	

Note: (a) As regards other activities, 100 per cent FDI is approved in alcohol distillation and brewing.

(b) FDI under the automatic route does not require any prior approval either by the government or the RBI. The investors are only required to notify the concerned regional office of the RBI within 30 days of receipt of inward remittances and file the required documents with that office within 30 days of issuance of shares to foreign investors. Under the approval route, proposals are considered in a time-bound and transparent manner by the FIPB. Approvals of composite proposals involving foreign investment/foreign technical collaboration are also granted on the recommendations of the FIPB.

(c) FIPB stands for Foreign Investment Promotion Board.

Source: *http://www.rbi.org.in/* (last accessed on 29/12/2013).

Appendix B

Table B.1

Socioeconomic Survey: A Snapshot

Firm	*Segment*	*Investment (US$)*	*Annual Turnover (US$)*	*Employment*	*R&D Centre*	*Manufacturing Centre*	*Exports*	*CSR Activity*
A	Software product development	N/A	1 billion	5800	Yes	N/A	Yes	Yes
B	IT solutions, services and support	N/A	2 billion	27,000	Yes	Yes, mainly assembly	Yes	Yes
C	IT services	N/A	0.12 billion	38,500	No	N/A	Yes	Yes
D	Pharmaceuticals	N/A	0.17 billion	4000	Yes	Yes	Yes	Yes
E	Pharmaceuticals	58 million	11 billion	540	Yes	Yes	N/A	Aligns business operations with social values
F	Direct selling FMCG—health, beauty and home care products	40 million	0.39 billion	2500 (direct and indirect) and indirect employment for 2000 persons	Yes	Yes, through seven third-party contract manufacturers	No	Yes
G	FMCG—oral care, toilet soap and shaving cream	N/A	230 million	1130	Yes	Yes	Yes	Yes
H	FMCG—beverages	2 billion	N/A	Direct employment to 25,000 people, and indirect employment to 150,000	Yes	Yes	Yes	Yes
I	Healthcare equipment	N/A	N/A	350	Yes	No	No	Not significant
J	IT and BPO services provider in healthcare segment	N/A	N/A	300	N/A	N/A	Yes	Not significant
K	Chemicals and additives	25 million	N/A	N/A	No	Yes	Yes	Yes
L	Automobiles	2 billion	N/A	11,500	Yes	Yes	Yes	Yes

Note: N/A: either not available or not applicable. Figures are approximate as they have been compiled from primary and secondary sources.

Source: Author's compilation.

Table B.2

Questionnaire for Socioeconomic Survey

1. What has been the history and nature of your company's investments (FDI) in India? Which segments and locations has your company made investments in?
2. What have been the determinants of your company's FDI in India?
3. How would you assess the Indian market vis-à-vis other markets where you have significant presence?
4. What has been the employment generated by your company in India? What would be the proportion of white to blue collar jobs generated? What is the proportion of women employed at these levels? What has been the nature of skill upgradation undertaken?
5. What has been the nature of technology transfer to India through your parent company? Do you have a R&D centre in India, if yes, has any technology developed from the centre been transferred elsewhere? Has your company transferred technology to any firm based in India? Please give examples.
6. What have been some of the 'best practices' introduced by your company? Have any of these practices been emulated by other Indian firms?
7. What percentage and nature of products/services generated in India by your company are exported? To which countries?
8. What is your perception of the socio-economic contribution of U.S. FDI to India and your company in particular?
9. How do you rate the support of the governments of your home country and that of the Government of India with regard to your investments in India?
10. What are the future investment plans of your company in India?
11. What are the major problems that your company has faced in the process of making FDI inflows and operations in India? These could pertain to the following aspects:
    - Approvals from government authorities
    - Visa issues
    - Labour laws
    - Repatriation of profits
    - Other operational problems
12. Are there any reform requirements that you would like to suggest to improve FDI attractiveness/inflows in India?
13. What are some examples of CSR practices followed by your company?

Appendix C

Questionnaires for Consumer Survey

Table C.1

Banking Sector

1. Name of respondent ____________________
2. Age profile ____________
3. Level of education – years of formal schooling ___________
4. Source of income a. Self b. employee – Indian, Multinational
5. How long have you been using banking services?___________
6. Which banks(s) do you use? please mention names
   (a) Indian ______________________________
   (b) Foreign______________________________
7. Why have you decided to use the bank(s) you are using?

Details	*Indian Banks*		*Foreign Banks*
Convenient location	Public	Private	
Safety of funds			
Bank reputation			
Efficient service			
Low service charge			

Which category of the banks mentioned above do you prefer? Please explain

8. Which of these banks offer lower interest rates to you?
9. Any dissatisfaction with the banking services that you are using

Dissatisfaction	*Indian Banks*		*Foreign Banks*
	Public	Private	

10. What is your assessment of the impact of US banks in India, for example, in terms of employment and financial inclusion?

Table C.2

FMCG Products

1. Monthly income of your family:

   Up to Rs. 20,000__________

   Rs. 20,000-40,000_________

   Greater than Rs. 40,000___________

2. Are you aware of these brands available in the market? If yes, put a tick mark. Also rank your preferences from 1-highest to 4-lowest

   Skin care:

   a) Pond's

   b) Garnier

   c) Fair & Lovely

   d) Amway

   e) Tupperware

   Hair care:

   a) Head & Shoulders

   b) Garnier

   c) Pantene

   d) Sunsilk

   e) Clinic Plus

   Detergent powder:

   a) Surf

   b) Tide

   c) Ariel

   d) Nirma

   e) 555

   Cold drinks:

   a) Pepsi

   b) Coca-Cola

   c) Fanta

   d) Mirinda

   e) Limca

Tooth paste:

a) Pepsodent

b) Colgate

c) Close-up

d) Promise

e) Neem

Packaged Food:

a) Kellogg's

b) Mohan

c) Heinz

d) Kissan

e) Kraft

3. Which of the products are the most used and for how long have you been using these brands?

   Skin care:

   a) Pond's

   b) Garnier

   c) Fair & Lovely

   d) Amway

   e) Tupperware

   Hair care:

   a) Head & Shoulders

   b) Garnier

   c) Pantene

   d) Sunsilk

   e) Clinic Plus

   Detergent powder:

   a) Surf

   b) Tide

   c) Ariel

   d) Nirma

   e) 555

Cold drinks:

a) Pepsi

b) Coca-Cola

c) Fanta

d) Mirinda

e) Limca

Tooth paste:

a) Pepsodent

b) Colgate

c) Close-up

d) Promise

e) Neem

Packaged Food:

a) Kellogg's

b) Mohan

c) Heinz

d) Kissan

e) Kraft

4. Are you satisfied with the quality of the above products?
5. How do you compare these products from US companies with similar ones from Indian companies in terms of quality, pricing, marketing, etc.
6. Would you switch over to other brands in case there are better deals in the market in terms of your preferences?
7. Do you think that the Government's decision to raise the limit of foreign direct investment (FDI) in multi-brand retail trading to 74 per cent from the present 51 per cent limit will impact consumption in any way? How?
8. What is your assessment of the impact of American FMCG products in India?

Table C.3

IT Sector

Questionnaire for Socioeconomic Survey of the IT Sector

1. Name of respondent
2. Age profile
3. Level of education – years of formal schooling
4. Gender
5. Source of income a. Self b. employee – Indian, Multinational
6. No. of members in household of which no. of dependents

---

7. Do you use any software products like Adobe, FireFox, Internet explorer for your business or at home?

   If the answer to the question above is yes, what products?
8. Have you bought these products from a licensed distributor or from the grey market?
9. What explains your reasons for the choice in the question above? Do you see any difference in the pricing pattern of licensed versus the grey market?
10. Do you feel that patenting of these software products has affected your decision to use the product?
11. Approximately, what percentage of your income do you spend on software products every year on yourself and those dependent on you (if any)?
12. Are you aware of any Indian software products/will you use these products?
13. What is your assessment of the impact of American software products in India?

Table C.4

Pharmaceuticals

1. Name of respondent
2. Age profile
3. Level of education – years of formal schooling
4. Gender
5. Source of income a. Self b. employee – Indian, Multinational
6. No. of members in household of which no. of dependents
7. Are you or anyone in your family inflicted with any life threatening disease or other disease such as cardio-vascular disorder or diabetes?
8. If the answer to the question above is yes, are you on a prescribed drug for curing the disease?
9. Do you consume drugs supplied by MNCs (e.g. Corex/Lipitor/Januvia) or those produced by Indian pharmaceutical companies?
10. Do you see any difference in the pricing pattern of MNCs and the Indian pharmas?
11. Do you feel that patenting of some drugs produced by the MNCs has affected you or someone in your family?
12. Approximately, what percentage of your income do you spend on healthcare every year on yourself and those dependent on you (if any)?
13. Do you think that price controls or abolition of patent protection act in the pharma industry augur well for your expenditure pattern on healthcare?
14. What is your assessment of the impact of MNC drugs (particularly American drugs) in India?